FELIX MENDELSSOHN

SYMPHONY No. 4

A major/A-Dur/La majeur
Op. 90
"Italian"

Edited by/Herausgegeben von
Boris von Haken

Ernst Eulenburg Ltd

London · Mainz · Madrid · New York · Paris · Prague · Tokyo · Toronto · Zürich

CONTENTS

Ernst Eulenburg Ltd
48 Great Marlborough Street
London W1F 7BB

PREFACE

In the Autumn of 1830 Felix Mendelssohn Bartholdy set off on a musical study tour, travelling to Italy in order to become more closely acquainted with a number of important artists, works of art and artistic institutions. Like many other musicians of his generation, he was deeply disappointed by the musical culture he found in Italy at that time. Outside the concert halls, however, Mendelssohn found inspiration. On 22 November 1830 he wrote from Rome to his teacher Carl Friedrich Zelter:

The greatest musical inspiration has come from things other than actual music: the ruins, the images of the joy of Nature.[1]

The first vague reference to the 'Italian' Symphony appears in a letter to his family, written from Rome on 20 December 1830: 'In the New Year I want to get back to writing instrumental music: several pieces for the pianoforte and perhaps one or the other of the symphonies I have floating around inside my head.'[2] One of the two symphonies to which Mendelssohn is alluding here is the 'Scottish' Symphony, not completed until 1842; the other is the 'Italian' Symphony. On 22 February 1831, while still in Rome, Mendelssohn reported on the composition of this symphony:

I find I am now able to compose with renewed vigour. The 'Italian Symphony' is progressing rapidly; it will be the happiest piece I have written – indeed, the ultimate in cheerfulness; for the Adagio I do not yet have any clear ideas, and I think I will save that for Naples.[3]

Here for the first time Mendelssohn refers to the work as the 'Italian' Symphony although, as with the 'Scottish' Symphony, he only used this description in letters to his family and friends,

but not in public. In spite of this announcement, the process of composition did not proceed without interruption. On 1 March Mendelssohn wrote:

The Italian (Symphony) I want to – indeed, will have to – save until I have seen Naples, for that will have its own part to play.[4]

In Naples, however, he did not continue work on the composition, working instead on the Ballade 'The first *Walpurgis* night'. Even when he stopped working on that piece, he did not immediately turn again to the 'Italian' Symphony.

Not until 20 months later, in November 1832, was Mendelssohn provided with a real impetus to continue with the composition, in the form of an invitation to compose three works for the Philharmonic Society in London. On 8 November William Watts, the Secretary of the Society, wrote with details of the commission:

I beg to transmit to you a Copy of a Resolution passed at a General Meeting of the Philharmonic Society, held on Monday Evening the 5th. 'Resolved, That Mr. Mendelssohn Bartholdy be requested to compose a Symphony, an Overture and a Vocal Piece for the Society, for which he be offered the sum of one hundred Guineas. The copyright of the said compositions to revert to the author after the expiration of two years; the Society reserving to itself the power of performing them at all times, and with the understanding that Mr. Mendelssohn Bartholdy be permitted to publish any arrangement of them, so soon as he may think fit, after their first performance at the Society's Concerts.'[5]

In his letter of reply of 28 November Mendelssohn accepted the commission. For a while he considered the idea of offering the Philharmonic Society the choice of either the 'Italian' Sym-

---

[1] Ernst Wolff, *Felix Mendelssohn Bartholdy* (Berlin, 1906), 87

[2] Paul and Carl Mendelssohn Bartholdy (eds.), *Briefe aus den Jahren 1830 bis 1847 von Felix Mendelssohn Bartholdy* (Leipzig, 1870), 78

[3] ibid., 93

[4] Letter to his family from Rome, dated 1 March, ibid., 94

[5] Letter from William Watts to Mendelssohn, dated 8 November 1832, in the Bodleian Library, Oxford *(GB-Ob* MS. M. D. M. d. 28, 72), quoted from John Michael Cooper, *Felix Mendelssohn Bartholdy and the Italian Symphony: Historical, Musical and Extramusical Perspectives* (diss. Duke University, 1994); in abbreviated form in Myles B. Foster, *History of the Philharmonic Society of London* (London, 1912), 111; George Hogarth, *The Philharmonic Society of London* (London, 1862), 59

phony or the 'Scottish'; since he found himself unable to complete the 'Scottish' Symphony at that point, he eventually decided upon the 'Italian' alone. Not until January 1833 did Mendelssohn again begin work on the 'Italian' Symphony, this time making rapid progress. On 13 March he finished the first draft of the MS and in a letter to the clergyman Albert Bauer he writes a first summary of the work:

My work, which has occasioned many doubts in me in recent times, is now finished and, contrary to my expectations, I think it has turned out well. I am pleased with the piece and, for what it is worth, I feel that it represents a step forward – and *that* is what counts. As long as I have this feeling, I know that I am alive and happy.[6]

At the end of April Mendelssohn travelled to London and handed over the MS score of the 'Italian' Symphony, together with two Overtures, to the Directors of the Philharmonic Society.[7] One of the overtures offered was that to 'Fair Melusine'. The other, which Mendelssohn offered, may have been the 'Trumpet Overture'. The vocal piece also commissioned – probably the concert aria 'Infelice', Op.94 – Mendelssohn did not manage to deliver until a year later.[8]

The first performance of the 'Italian' Symphony took place at the 6th Monday concert of the season, on 13 May 1833, at the Hanover Square Rooms in London. Mendelssohn also performed in this concert as the soloist in Mozart's D minor Piano Concerto. Works by Haydn, Pixis, Rossini, De Beriot, Meyerbeer and Weber also figured on the programme. The programme notes for the concert give the names of both the leader of the orchestra, Charles Weichsell, and Mendelssohn, the 'conductor'. In accordance with the performance practice of the Philharmonic Society at that time, it was the role of the 'conductor' to accompany the orchestra from the piano and to bring them in at the beginning of each movement, while the 'leader' marked the beat and set the tempo. The chief responsibility for directing the orchestra thus lay with the 'leader'.[9] This was not what Mendelssohn had in mind, however: he decided that he alone would conduct, using a baton.[10] The performance was a great success, as the reviews published in the London journals *The Harmonicon* and *The Athenaeum* attest.[11] The audience insisted upon having the second movement played through again. Moscheles wrote in his diary of that evening:

On 13 May Mendelssohn was the jewel of the concert, presenting his wonderful A major Symphony for the first time, to thunderous applause.[12]

A week after this concert Mendelssohn left London and travelled to Düsseldorf for the Lower Rhineland Music Festival. The original score of the 'Italian' Symphony remained in London for the next few years. Only three further performances of the 'Italian' Symphony took place during Mendelssohn's lifetime, all of them in London by the Philharmonic Society: on 2 June 1834, 15 May 1837 and 18 June 1838. In the year of its first performance Mendelssohn was already planning to publish the symphony. On 6 September 1833 he wrote to Julius Schubring:

My latest Symphony has been performed in England too; people enjoyed it, and now the Hebrides Overture is to be printed, followed by the Symphony.[13]

Mendelssohn did not, however, realize this plan, nor is there any evidence of correspondence

6 Paul and Carl Mendelssohn Bartholdy (eds.), op. cit., 272
7 See below in the notes on the revised score: source 1
8 The first performance of 'Fair Melusine' took place on 7 April 1834, that of the concert aria on 19 May 1834. The 'Trumpet Overture' had its first performance on 10 June 1833 in London. The programme notes state inaccurately: 'composed expressly for the Philharmonic Society, and first time of performance'. This piece had been performed for the first time as a 'Festival Overture' on 26 May 1833 in Düsseldorf.
9 The programme notes published by the Philharmonic Society up to 1846 when Michael Costas took sole charge – always attribute musical direction to two people. cf. George Grove, article entitled 'Conductor' in George Grove (ed.), *A Dictionary of Music and Musicians* (London, 1890), Vol.1, 389–390.
10 cf. the review in *The Morning Post*, 16 May 1833; after that season other conductors with the Philharmonic Society followed Mendelsohn's lead, cf. Adam Carse: *The Orchestra from Beethoven to Berlioz* (Cambridge, 1948), 317–340
11 *Harmonicon* Vol.11 (1833), 134; *The Athenaeum* No. 288 (1833), 316; *The Times* did not print a review.
12 Charlotte Moscheles (ed.), *Aus Moscheles Leben. Nach Briefen und Tagebüchern* (Leipzig, 1872/73), Vol.1, 264
13 Paul and Carl Mendelssohn Bartholdy (eds.), op. cit., 275

with publishers to indicate that he took any actual steps towards publication.[14] In June 1834 Mendelssohn again began work on the 'Italian' Symphony. In Düsseldorf he was visited by his old friend Dr Hermann Franck, for whom he wrote out the second, third and fourth movements from memory, while undertaking numerous revisions and improvements.[15] At about the same time his sister Fanny Hensel asked him to write out and send her the theme of the second movement.[16] On 5 July 1834 Mendelssohn sent the whole second movement of the symphony in the revised version. The present whereabouts of this MS are unknown. What has been preserved, though, is Fanny's letter of reply, which expresses reservations about those modifications:

I don't like the changes in the first melody at all; why did you make it? Was it to avoid the many A's? But the melody was natural and lovely. I don't agree with the other changes either; however, I am still not familiar enough with the rest of the movement to be able to render a reasonable judgement. Overall I feel you are only too ready to change a successful piece later on merely because one thing or another pleases you more then. It is always tough, however, for someone to become accustomed to a new version once he knows the old one. Bring the old version along with you when you come and then we can argue about it.[17]

In the ensuing months Mendelssohn also undertook to write out a revised version of the first movement. It was his intention to revise the piece thoroughly – possibly even to compose a new movement, but this he did not accomplish. On 16 February 1835 he wrote to Klingemann:

I have also been wrestling with the first movement of the A major symphony and I just cannot get it right – in any case, it will have to be changed radically – perhaps completely rewritten – but I do have my doubts about writing a new movement.[18]

This is the last known documentation of Mendelssohn working on the composition of his 'Italian' Symphony. In spite of being urged several times by his sister to do so, he did not go on to complete the work. Then on 23 December 1837 Ignaz Moscheles wrote to Mendelssohn asking him to provide the new version for a performance by the Philharmonic Society:

You promised us your new arrangement of the A major Symphony and we will hold you to your word; but please do not make us wait long. It is my favourite and I feel as though I were about to meet a lovely girl in a new dress and doubt whether I could possibly like her better than before. Nous verrons – nous entendrons.[19]

Mendelssohn did not respond even to these entreaties. On 20 October 1840 he received a letter from William Watts, the Secretary of the Philharmonic Society, reminding him of his supposed promise to revise the first movement:

They [the directors of the Philharmonic Society] likewise desire me to remind you of your proposed intention of writing a new first movement to your Symphony in A which they are very anxious to possess when finished.[20]

Mendelssohn took this request as an affront.[21] His actual letter of reply has not been preserved.

[14] George A.MacFarren's report in *The Musical World*, Vol.30 (1852) No.41, 641 and the programme booklet of the Philharmonic Society for 21 June 1875 both suggest that Mendelssohn had had an arrangement for piano duet rejected by the London publishers Cramer & Co., but this seems very unlikely. In a review dated 1852 MacFarren wrongly assumed the arrangement for piano duet published in 1851 by Ewer & Co. to be Mendelssohn's own arrangement. In fact the 1851 edition was based upon the edition published in that same year by Breitkopf & Härtel: 'Symphony No.4 for Orchestra by Felix Mendelssohn Bartholdy, arranged for piano duet', plate number 8361. This arrangement was by Julius Rietz. cf. list of publications issued by the music publishers Breitkopf & Härtel in Leipzig. Complete to the end of 1891, Vol.1, 398
[15] See below: notes on revised score, source 2
[16] Letter from Fanny Hensel, dated 18 June 1834, in: Marcia J. Citron (ed.), *The Letters of Fanny Hensel to Felix Mendelssohn* (Pendragon Press, 1987), 471
[17] Letter from Fanny Hensel, undated (c. 1 August) in: Marcia J. Citron (ed.), ibid., 151
[18] Karl Klingemann (ed.): *Felix Mendelssohn-Bartholdys Briefwechsel mit Legationsrat Karl Klingemann in London* (Essen, 1909), 171
[19] Felix Moscheles (ed.): *Briefe von Felix Mendelssohn-Bartholdy an Ignaz und Charlotte Moscheles* (Leipzig, 1888), 150
[20] Letter from W. Watts, dated 20 October 1840, in the Bodleian Library, Oxford *(GB-Ob* MS. M. D. M. d. 38, 103), quoted from John Michael Cooper, op. cit.
[21] cf. Mendelssohn's letter to Klingemann of 26 October 1840, in: *Felix Mendelssohn-Bartholdys Briefwechsel mit Legationsrat Karl Klingemann in London* (Essen, 1909), 248–250

On the back of Watts' letter, however, he sketched out an answer in English:

I also was not aware that I communicated to the Philh. Soc. My intention of writing a new 1st movt. to my Symphony in A. Although I once thought it I cannot tell you [originally: do not know] at present whether or when I shall do so.[22]

Following this, Charles Neate, one of the Directors of the Philharmonic Society, wrote to Mendelssohn in order to resolve matters:

I very much regret to find, by a communication from Moscheles, that there has been some misunderstanding between you and the Philharmonic Society, on the subject of your Symphony in A. It appears that you were surprised at the question 'Whether you had written a new movement.' I do not wonder at your surprise, as it seems you have forgotten the conversation with me, on our way home from Mrs Shaw's[23] in Berner's Street [,] when upon my observing that we – the Philharmonic – were going to perform your Symphony in A – you replied, ['] No! Do not perform it again yet, as I wish to make a new first (or last, I forget which) movement ['] and therefore – it was not performed.[24]

Here again, the only record of Mendelssohn's reply – in English – is on the back of Neate's letter:

I do not know the communication of Moscheles which you refer to in the beginning but I felt indeed some astonishment to receive and [sic] invitation from this Soc[.] of doing so. I confess even that your letter does not alter my impression in that respect, for I am perfectly aware that I had once such an idea; nor do I think that if you had communicated this conversation of ours to the Society, (for which I really think it was not intended) the effect would have been, as you say in your letter, that the performances of this Symph[.] have been stopped, and of this I would indeed not have felt astonished nor would I have complained of it. But it appears that neither I nor you considered that conversation of ours as anything like a message for

the Philh., for I find a year after it [had] taken place the Symph. has been performed at the Philh. Soc., which circumstance you seem to have forgotten.[25] Accordingly as you had not told the Philh. in June 1838 of what I might have said to you in September 1837, it must either not have been intended for the Soc., or you must give me credit for some astonishment (to find the mention of our [conversation] of 1840 of which I had not given them a direct notice [)]. But all this really refers to the invitation of a new movt. to an old composition of mine, and it is quite erroneous and far from my true feelings if you suppose in your letter that I wish for any explanations why this Symph. has not been performed. Of such a thing I shall never complain, nor express any regret for indeed I always considered it as a natural [crossed out: and welcome] consequence of the true value of a composition & you will recollect how often I expressed to you & others that I am far from satisfied with this, and indeed many other Compositions of mine.[26]

This correspondence was concluded with a letter of apology from William Watts and Charles Neate on 19 March 1841.[27] The 'Italian' Symphony thus remained unfinished and was not performed again at any later date during Mendelssohn's lifetime. The first posthumous performance was given at the request of Queen Victoria on 13 March 1848 by the Philharmonic Society in London. The first performance in Germany took place, after a long period of preparation, on 1 November 1849 at the Leipzig Gewandhaus. The score was printed and published in the complete version in 1851 by Breitkopf & Härtel, Leipzig, as 'Symphony No.4 [...], Op.90, No.19 of the posthumously published works', by Mendelssohn's literary/musical executors: Ferdinand David, Moritz Hauptmann, Ignaz Moscheles and Julius Rietz.

---

[22] ibid.

[23] This conversation took place during the first weeks of September 1837 following a visit to the contralto Mary Shaw (1814–1876).

[24] Letter dated 18 Jan. 1841 in the Bodleian Library, Oxford (GB-Ob MS. M. D. M. d. 39, 24), quoted from John Michael Cooper, op. cit.

[25] This refers to a performance on 18 June 1838 with Moscheles as 'leader'.

[26] Bodleian Library, Oxford (GB-Ob MS. M. D. M. d. 39, 133), in: John Michael Cooper, op. cit.

[27] ibid.

The Sources

The following original documents have survived as sources for Mendelssohn's 'Italian' Symphony.

1. A complete autograph score in the possession of the Staatsbibliothek zu Berlin – Preußischer Kulturbesitz, Mendelssohn Archive (*D-B* Mus. ms. autogr. Mendelssohn 27, pages 1–99). (AUT).

There are two page-numbering systems, in an unknown hand, beginning on the title-page and continuing through all four movements. Here the page numbers are only written on the recto pages. Page numbering in Mendelssohn's handwriting, for the first movement alone, beginning on page 3, numbered as page 1, continues through to page 48, numbered as page 44.

Two pages each had another piece of paper stuck over them by Mendelssohn, concealing the original version. The glued pages are included in the first numbering system: at the end of the first movement bar 98ff. is on page 46 in the original version, with page 47 blank and page 48 offering the final version. In the fourth movement bars 97–104 are on page 77 in the original version, with page 78 blank and page 79 offering the final version. Vertical format, 16 staves. Various kinds of paper. On the title-page, in Mendelssohn's handwriting, *Sinfonia für ganzes Orchester*, with (*op.90*) added by another hand. Page 2 is blank, with MS continuing from page 3 onwards. On page 3 inscribed in the top left-hand corner *Sinfonia*; in the top right-hand corner there is the abbreviation *H. D. m.* (Hilf Du mir – Lord be my helper). The last page was marked by Mendelssohn with the date *Berlin den 13 März 1833*.

AUT is the score which Mendelssohn used for the first performance on 13 May 1833 in London. The score bears the date of completion 13 March 1833. On 10 April

Mendelssohn had the score bound in Berlin.[28] Two days after his arrival in London on 27 April he informed the Directors of the Philharmonic Society that the score was now available.[29] On 1 May the entry appears in Mendelssohn's diary: 'Finished looking through symph[ony] in eve[ning]', on 11 May, the day of the first rehearsal, the entry: 'parts ch[ecked] early'.[30] After the first performance the score remained in London, possibly initially with the Philharmonic Society. Then it was left in the hands of Ignaz Moscheles, as is clear from a letter written by Moscheles to Mendelssohn in the year 1837.[31] The score was later returned to Mendelssohn; it is not known exactly when. It appears in the list he compiled in 1844 of all his own musical writings.[32]

2. Autograph sketches in the possession of the Bodleian Library, Oxford (*GB-Ob* MS. M. D. M. b. 5, Fols. 136r–146v). Folio numbering by an unknown hand. These sketches contain fully scored material from the first, third and fourth movements. They are closely related to AUT and may have been written during the reworking of AUT.[33]

3. Manuscript copy in the possession of the British Library, London, on loan from the Royal Philharmonic Society (*GB-Lbm* Loan 4/290). No folio or page num-

28 cf. Letter from Mendelssohn dated 10 April 18[33] in: Karl Klingemann (ed.): *Felix Mendelssohn-Bartholdys Briefwechsel mit Legationsrat Karl Klingemann in London* (Essen, 1909), 115
29 Letter to William Watts in: Myles B. Foster, *History of the Philharmonic Society of London* (London, 1862), 60
30 Diary in the Bodleian Library, Oxford (*GB-Ob* MS. M. D. M. g. 4), quoted from John Michael Cooper, op. cit.
31 Letter dated 23 Dec. 1837 in: Felix Moscheles (ed.): *Briefe von Felix Mendelssohn-Bartholdy an Ignaz und Charlotte Moscheles* (Leipzig, 1888), 150
32 'Mendelssohn's 1844 List of his Music' in: Peter Ward Jones (ed.), *Catalogue of the Mendelssohn Papers in the Bodleian Library*, Oxford, Vol.III, 292
33 A detailed evaluation and description of these rough sketches is offered by John Michael Cooper in: '"Aber eben dieser Zweifel": A New Look at Mendelssohn's "Italian" Symphony', in: *19th Century Music*, Vol.15, No.3 (1992), 169–187

bering (160 pages). (BL).

Horizontal format, 16 staves. Pages 1–44 have *W.GOODWIN, 4, UPPER WEL-LINGTON ST.,* printed in the bottom left-hand corner and *COVENT GARDEN* in the bottom right-hand corner. On the title-page stands *Sinfonie No4* (originally *Sinfonie No2*) Mendelssohn Score 1848. Writing is continuous from pages 2 to 158.

At the end of each movement there is a blank page.

Manuscript written by the copyist William Goodwin. Corrections and subsequent additions by William Sterndale Bennett. On page 33 part of the music has the comment added *? something wanted WSB.*

BL is a copy which the Philharmonic Society had made for the first posthumous performance of the 'Italian' Symphony on 13 March 1848 in London. In the *Directors Minutes* of the Society of 13 February 1848 appears the entry: 'ordered, that a score of Mendelssohn's Symphony in A, No.2, be made forthwith'.[34] The following day, the copyist William Goodwin was commissioned by the Secretary of the Society, G.W. Budd, to produce such a copy: 'The Directors wish to have a Score made by next Sunday of Mendelssohn's Symphony in A – No2. If you let me have it late on Saturday night it will do.'[35] The Directors received the score by the appointed time. In the Directors Minutes of 20 February 1848 appear instructions for the following to be included in a letter to William Goodwin: 'The Directors feel much pleased with your punctuality in sending the Symphony.'[36]

Goodwin's copy cannot have been based on AUT, as the original score was among Mendelssohn's effects in Leipzig at the time. Thus the only possible explanation is that this copy of the score was put together from the orchestral parts used for the first performance, the property of the Philharmonic Society. It is not known what became of those orchestral parts.[37]

4. A revised autograph score of the second, third and fourth movements, in the possession of the Staatsbibliothek zu Berlin – Preußischer Kulturbesitz, Mendelssohn Archive (*D-B* Mus. ms. autogr. Mendelssohn 28, pages 5–58)

The pages have been numbered by an unidentified hand on the recto side alone. One page had another page stuck over it by Mendelssohn, thus concealing the original version. The pages that are glued together are counted in the numbering system: in the second movement, bars 77ff., the original version appears on page 10, with page 11 left blank and page 12 giving the final version. Vertical format, 16 systems. On page 5 the abbreviation *H. D. m.* (Hilf Du mir/Lord be my helper) appears in the top right-hand corner. This revised score was written out in June 1834 in Düsseldorf. On 26 June 1834 Mendelssohn wrote to Ignaz and Charlotte Moscheles:

Dr Franck, with whom you are acquainted, recently came to Düsseldorf, and I wished to be able to show him a few things in my A major symphony; as it is not now in my possession, I began to write out the Andante again, and in so doing came across so many errata that it caught my interest and I went on to write out the Minuet and the Finale too, but with many very necessary improve-

---

[34] In the possession of the British Library, London. On loan from the Royal Philharmonic Society (Loan 48. 2. 4. (1848))

[35] Entry made on 14 February 1848 in the copy book of the Philharmonic Society, in the possession of the British Library, London, on loan from the Royal Philharmonic Society: Copies of Letters 1846–49 (Loan 48. 6. 2.)

[36] In the possession of the British Library. London, on loan from the Royal Philharmonic Society (Loan 48. 2. 4. (1848))

[37] cf. for this MS see: Peter Ward Jones: 'Mendelssohn Scores in the Library of the Philharmonic Society', in: Schmidt, Christian Martin (ed.): *Felix Mendelssohn Bartholdy*, Kongress-Bericht (Berlin, 1994; Wiesbaden/Leipzig/ Paris, 1997), 64–75

ments; whenever I came upon such a detail, my thoughts were of you, who never uttered a word of criticism to me about the music, where you must have been far more clearly and better aware of those weaknesses than I am now. Only the first movement have I left as it was, for if I were to start on it, I fear I would have to change the whole theme from bar 4 onwards, that is, rewrite practically the entire movement, and I really don't have the time for it just now. I am not happy with the dominant in bar 4; I think it should be a seventh (A-G).[38]

Again in a letter to Klingemann two days later Mendelssohn mentioned this modification of the second, third and fourth movements in the score: 'When I read your kind comments on my symphony I immediately set about writing out and revising the last three movements for Franck; I wish I could just play them to you, for they are much improved. Particularly Nos.2 and 3.'[39] A letter to Ignaz and Charlotte Moscheles indicates that Mendelssohn was not yet envisaging rewriting the first movement at that time. This is borne out by his abbreviation *H. D. m.* on page 5 of the score, always used by Mendelssohn to mark the beginning of a new composition.[40]

Editorial Principles

Mendelssohn never completed the composition of his 'Italian' Symphony. Contrary to his original intention, he did not publish a printed score of the work. He only did part of the thorough reworking which he had intended. The documents still in existence do not establish conclusively

whether the revised scoring of the second, third and fourth movements represents the final version of those four movements. Mendelssohn did not actually use the revised and incomplete score of 1834 for a performance. Nor is it possible to gauge the extent to which Mendelssohn would have revised or possibly even rewritten the first movement of the symphony. What remains of his correspondence with the Philharmonic Society from the years 1840/41 shows clearly, though, that Mendelssohn was not intent upon abandoning this symphony – which he had already presented to the public in a concert performance, while he may not have supported further performances. This present edition shows the 'Italian' Symphony in its 'London' version, as performed in the concert hall. It thus corresponds in the main to the version published in 1851 as 'Symphony No.4 [...], Op.90, No.19 of the posthumous work'.

In accordance with this decision AUT forms the basis for the present edition, with missing details supplied by reference to BL. The revised score of the second, third and fourth movements of 1834 has not been used, in order to avoid producing too eclectic an edition.

The positioning of phrase marks and of dynamic and tempo markings in AUT is often ambiguous, due to haste in writing and numerous later additions. Such instances are indicated with individual textual notes.

There are also many discrepancies with regard to phrasing, dynamics and tempo indications. Mendelssohn's style of writing has been adhered to in principle.

The strokes used in AUT and BL to indicate staccato markings are represented as narrow wedges (') in this edition. In a small number of cases the placing of staccato dots and staccato strokes has been adjusted for the sake of consistency. Details of such adjustments are given in the individual footnotes. Those places where the distinction between staccato dots and staccato lines is unclear in AUT are likewise indicated in the footnotes.

Boris von Haken
Translation: J. S. Rushworth

[38] Felix Moscheles (ed.), op. cit., 95–96
[39] Letter to Klingemann, dated 26 June 1834, in: Karl Klingemann (ed.), op. cit., 135
[40] A philological analysis of this manuscript is offered by John Michael Cooper in: '"Aber eben dieser Zweifel": A New Look at Mendelssohn's "Italian" Symphony', in: *19th Century Music*, Vol.15, No.3 (1992), 169–187, and Wulf Konold: *Die Symphonien Felix Mendelssohn Bartholdys – Untersuchungen zu Werkgestalt und Formstruktur* (Laaber, 1992), 394–413

VORWORT

Felix Mendelssohn Bartholdy beginnt im Herbst 1830 eine musikalische Bildungsreise nach Italien, um bedeutende Künstler, Kunstwerke und Kunstinstitutionen kennenzulernen. Doch wie viele andere Musiker seiner Generation ist er von der damaligen Musikkultur Italiens tief enttäuscht. Mendelssohn findet dagegen außerhalb der Konzertsäle Inspiration. Am 22. November 1830 schreibt er aus Rom an seinen ehemaligen Lehrer Carl Friedrich Zelter:

Auch verdanke ich dem, was nicht die eigentliche, unmittelbare Musik ist: den Ruinen, den Bildern der Heiterkeit der Natur, am meisten Musik.[1]

Der erste noch vage Hinweis auf die „Italienische Sinfonie" findet sich in einem Brief aus Rom an seine Familie vom 20. Dezember 1830: „Nach Neujahr will ich mich wieder an die Instrumentalmusik machen, mehreres für's Clavier und vielleicht noch eine oder die andere Symphonie; denn mir spuken zwei im Kopfe herum."[2] Eine der beiden Sinfonien, an welche Mendelssohn hier denkt, ist die erst 1842 vollendete „Schottische", die andere ist die „Italienische". Am 22. Februar 1831, immer noch in Rom, berichtet Mendelssohn von der Komposition dieser Sinfonie:

Überhaupt geht es mit dem Componieren jetzt wieder frisch. Die „italienische Symphonie" macht große Fortschritte; es wird das lustigste Stück, das ich gemacht habe, namentlich das letzte; für's Adagio hab' ich noch nichts Bestimmtes und glaube, ich will es mir für Neapel aufsparen.[3]

Hier bezeichnet Mendelssohn dieses Werk erstmals als „Italienische Sinfonie", doch er wird diese Beschreibung wie im Falle der „Schottischen" nur in der Korrespondenz mit seiner Familie und Freunden, dagegen nicht in der Öf-

fentlichkeit verwenden. Trotz der Ankündigung gerät der Kompositionsprozess wieder ins Stocken. Am 1. März schreibt er:

Die italienische (Sinfonie) will und muß ich mir aussparen, bis ich Neapel gesehen habe, denn das wird mitspielen.[4]

Er setzt jedoch auch in Neapel die Komposition nicht fort, sondern arbeitet an der Ballade „Die erste Walpurgisnacht". Auch nachdem er dieses Werk wieder zurückgelegt hat, befasst er sich zunächst nicht mehr mit der „Italienischen Sinfonie".

Den entscheidenden Anstoß die Komposition fortzuführen und zu vollenden erhält Mendelssohn erst 20 Monate später im November 1832 durch das Angebot, drei Werke für die Philharmonic Society in London zu komponieren. Am 8. November übermittelt William Watts, der Sekretär der Gesellschaft, den Kompositionsauftrag:

Gestatten Sie mir, Ihnen eine Abschrift eines Beschlusses zukommen zu lassen, der bei einer Vollversammlung der Philharmonischen Gesellschaft am Montag Abend dem 5. gefasst wurde. „Es wurde beschlossen, dass Herr Mendelssohn Bartholdy beauftragt wird eine Sinfonie, eine Ouvertüre und ein Vokalstück für die Gesellschaft zu komponieren, wofür ihm ein Honorar von 100 Guineen angeboten wird. Das Urheberrecht an besagten Kompositionen fällt nach Ablauf von zwei Jahren an den Autor zurück; wobei sich die Gesellschaft das Recht vorbehält, die Werke jederzeit aufzuführen, und mit dem Einvernehmen, dass Herrn Mendelssohn Bartholdy gestattet wird, sie nach ihrer Uraufführung in den Konzerten der Gesellschaft in jedweder Form zu veröffentlichen, sobald er dies für angebracht hält." [Originalzitat im englischen Vorwort][5]

---

[1] Wolff, Ernst: *Felix Mendelssohn Bartholdy*, Berlin 1906, S. 87.
[2] Mendelssohn Bartholdy, Paul/Mendelssohn Bartholdy, Carl (Hg.): *Briefe aus den Jahren 1830 bis 1847 von Felix Mendelssohn Bartholdy*, Leipzig 1870, S. 78.
[3] Ebda., S. 93.
[4] Brief vom 1. März aus Rom an seine Familie, ebda., S. 94.
[5] Brief von William Watts an Mendelssohn vom 8. November 1832 in Bodleian Library, Oxford (*GB-Ob* MS. M. D. M. d. 28, 72), zitiert nach Cooper, John Michael: *Felix Mendelssohn Bartholdy and the Italian Symphony: Historical, Musical, and Extramusical Perspectives*, Diss. Duke University 1994; in gekürzter Form in: Foster, Myles B.: *History of the Philharmonic Society of London*, London 1912, S. 111; Hogarth, George: *The Philharmonic Society of London*, London 1862, S. 59.

In seinem Antwortschreiben vom 28. November nimmt Mendelssohn den Kompositionsauftrag an. Zeitweilig erwägt er, der Philharmonic Society neben der „Italienischen Sinfonie" auch die „Schottische" zur Auswahl anzubieten. Da er die „Schottische Sinfonie" zu diesem Zeitpunkt nicht vollenden kann, entscheidet er sich letztendlich alleine für die „Italienische". Erst im Januar 1833 beginnt Mendelssohn wieder mit der Arbeit an dieser Sinfonie, die nun rasche Fortschritte macht. Am 13. März schließt er das Manuskript zunächst ab, und in einem Brief vom 6. April an den Pfarrer Albert Bauer findet sich bereits ein erstes Resümee seines Werkes:

Meine Arbeit, an der ich in der vorigen Zeit manche Zweifel hatte, ist beendigt und hat mich wider Erwarten, jetzt wo ich sie übersehe, selbst gefreut. Ich glaube, es ist ein gutes Stück geworden, und es sei wie es wolle, so fühle ich, daß ein Fortschritt darin ist, und nur *darauf* kommt es an. So lange ich dies Gefühl habe, weiß ich, daß ich lebe und glücklich bin.[6]

Ende April reist Mendelssohn nach London und übergibt das Autograph der „Italienischen Sinfonie" zusammen mit zwei Ouvertüren an die Direktoren der Philharmonic Society.[7] Eine der vorgelegten Ouvertüren ist die zum „Märchen von der schönen Melusine". Die andere, welche Mendelssohn offeriert, ist möglicherweise die „Trompeten-Ouvertüre". Das ebenfalls bestellte Vokalstück, es wird die Konzertarie „Infelice" op. 94 sein, kann Mendelssohn erst mit einjähriger Verspätung abliefern.[8]

Die Uraufführung der „Italienischen Sinfonie" findet im sechsten Montags-Konzert der Saison am 13. Mai 1833 in den *Hanover Square Rooms* in London statt. Mendelssohn tritt in diesem Konzert auch als Pianist mit dem d-Moll Klavierkonzert von Mozart auf. Des Weiteren stehen

Werke von Haydn, Pixis, Rossini, De Beriot, Meyerbeer und Weber auf dem Programm. Der Tageszettel des Konzertes gibt eine Doppeldirektion an: der „leader" des Orchesters ist der Konzertmeister Charles Weichsell, Mendelssohn der „conductor". Entsprechend der zu dieser Zeit üblichen Aufführungspraxis der Philharmonic Society, war es die Aufgabe des „conductor" das Orchester vom Klavier aus zu begleiten und die Einsätze für den Beginn der Sätze zu geben, während der „leader" Takt und Tempo anzeigte. Das Übergewicht der Dirigiertätigkeit lag somit bei dem „leader" des Orchesters.[9] Dies entsprach jedoch nicht den Intentionen Mendelssohns, der sich über die Gepflogenheit hinwegsetzte und das Orchester an diesem Tag alleine mit dem Taktstock dirigierte.[10] Die Aufführung war ein großer Erfolg, wie die Kritiken in den Londoner Musikzeitungen *Harmonicon* und *The Athenaeum* belegen.[11] Der zweite Satz musste auf Wunsch des Publikums wiederholt werden. Mendelssohns Freund, der Pianist Ignaz Moscheles, schrieb zu diesem Abend in seinem Tagebuch:

Am 13. Mai war Mendelssohn der Juwel des Concerts, indem er seine herrliche A-Dur-Symphonie zum ersten Mal mit dem rauschendsten Beifall gab.[12]

Eine Woche nach diesem Konzert verlässt Mendelssohn London und reist zum Niederrheinischen Musikfest nach Düsseldorf. Das Autograph der „Italienischen Sinfonie" verbleibt in den nächsten Jahren in London. Es finden zu Mendelssohns Lebzeiten nur drei weitere Aufführungen der „Italienischen Sinfonie" statt, alle in London durch die Philharmonic Society: Am 2. Juni 1834, 15. Mai 1837 und 18. Juni 1838. Noch im Jahr der Uraufführung plant Mendels-

---

[6] Mendelssohn Bartholdy, Paul/Mendelssohn Bartholdy, Carl (Hg.), ebda., S. 272.
[7] Siehe unten Revisionsbericht zu Quelle 1.
[8] Die Uraufführung des „Märchens von der schönen Melusine" erfolgt am 7. April 1834, die der Konzertarie am 19. Mai 1834. Die „Trompeten-Ouvertüre" wurde am 10. Juni 1833 in London aufgeführt. Der Tageszettel gibt irrtumlich an: „ausdrücklich für die Philharmonic Society komponiert und zum ersten Mal aufgeführt". Als „Festouvertüre" ist dieses Werk am 26. Mai 1833 in Düsseldorf uraufgeführt worden.

[9] Die Tageszettel der Philharmonic Society nennen bis 1846, dem Amtsantritt Michael Costas, ausschließlich die Doppeldirektion. Vgl. Grove, George: Artikel „Conductor" in: Grove, George (Hg.): *A Dictionary of Music and Musicians*, London 1890, Bd. 1, S. 389/390.
[10] Vgl. die Rezension in: *The Morning Post*, 16. Mai 1833; seit dieser Saison folgten auch andere Dirigenten der Philharmonic Society dem Vorbild Mendelssohns, vgl. Carse, Adam: *The Orchestra from Beethoven to Berlioz*, Cambridge 1948, S. 317–340.
[11] *Harmonicon*, Bd. 11 (1833), S. 134; *The Athenaeum*, Nr. 288 (1833), S. 316; in *The Times* erschien keine Rezension.
[12] Moscheles, Charlotte (Hg.): *Aus Moscheles Leben. Nach Briefen und Tagebüchern*, Leipzig 1872/73, Bd. 1, S. 264.

sohn eine Veröffentlichung der Sinfonie. Am 6. September 1833 schreibt er an Julius Schubring:

Auch meine neue Symphonie habe ich in England aufgeführt, und die Menschen haben sich dran gefreut, und nun werden die Hebriden gedruckt, und dann die Symphonie.[13]

Mendelssohn hat jedoch dieses Vorhaben nicht in die Tat umgesetzt; es sind auch keine Briefwechsel mit Verlegern bekannt, welche konkrete Schritte Mendelssohns für eine Veröffentlichung belegen.[14] Im Juni 1834 befasst sich Mendelssohn erneut mit der „Italienischen Sinfonie". In Düsseldorf besucht ihn sein langjähriger Freund Dr. Hermann Franck, für welchen er aus dem Gedächtnis den zweiten, dritten und vierten Satz aufschreibt und dabei noch zahlreiche Revisionen und Verbesserungen vornimmt.[15] Zur gleichen Zeit bittet ihn seine Schwester Fanny Hensel, ihr das Thema des zweiten Satzes aufzuschreiben und zuzusenden.[16] Mendelssohn schickt am 5. Juli 1834 den vollständigen zweiten Satz der Sinfonie in der überarbeiteten Version. Der Verbleib dieses Autographen ist unbekannt. Erhalten ist jedoch Fannys Antwortschreiben, in dem sie sich skeptisch gegenüber dieser Überarbeitung äußert:

Die Aenderung in der ersten Melodie gefällt mir nicht recht, warum hast Du sie gemacht? Um das viele a zu vermeiden? Die Melodie war aber natürlich u. schön. Die folgenden Veränderungen wollten mir auch nicht recht munden, indeß habe ich den weiteren Verlauf des Stückes doch nicht genau genug im Kopf, um eigentlich darüber urtheilen zu können. Im Ganzen glaub ich, gehst Du zu leicht daran, ein einmal gelungenes Stück später umzuarbeiten, blos weil Dir dies u. jenes dann besser gefällt. Es ist doch immer eine nüßliche Sache, u. wer sich einmal an eine Version gewöhnt hat, geht schwer daran, eine Abweichung zu dulden. Bring mir doch das Alte mit, wenn Du herkommst, dann können wir drüber disputieren.[17]

Mendelssohn befasst sich in den folgenden Monaten auch mit der Revision des ersten Satzes. Er beabsichtigt hier eine umfassende Überarbeitung, möglicherweise sogar die Komposition eines neuen Satzes, was ihm jedoch nicht gelingt. Am 16. Februar 1835 schreibt er an Klingemann:

Auch am ersten Stück der a-dur Sinfonie knabbere ich und kann es nicht recht kriegen – ganz anders werden muss es auf jedem Fall – vielleicht ganz neu – aber eben dieser Zweifel stört mich bei einem neuen Stück.[18]

Dies ist die letzte bekannte Quelle, welche eine kompositorische Auseinandersetzung Mendelssohns mit seiner „Italienischen Sinfonie" belegt. Auch trotz der mehrfachen Aufforderung seiner Schwester vollendet er dieses Werk nicht.

Am 23. Dezember 1837 schreibt wiederum Ignaz Moscheles an Mendelssohn mit der Bitte, die neue Fassung für eine Aufführung durch die Philharmonic Society vorzulegen:

Du hast uns Deine A dur-Symphonie in Deiner neuen Bearbeitung versprochen, und wir halten Dich beim Wort, nur bitte, laß uns nicht lange warten. Sie ist mein Liebling und es kommt mir vor, als sollte ich einem schönen Mädchen in einem neuen Kleid begegnen, und ich zweifelte, ob sie mir noch besser als früher gefallen könne. Nous verrons – nous entendrons.[19]

Mendelssohn kommt auch diesem Ersuchen nicht nach. Am 20. Oktober 1840 erhält er ein Schreiben von William Watts, dem Sekretär der Philharmonic Society, der ihn an sein vermeint-

---

[13] Mendelssohn Bartholdy, Paul/Mendelssohn Bartholdy, Carl (Hg.), ebda., S. 275.
[14] George A. MacParrens Bericht in: *The Musical World*, Bd. 30 (1852), Nr. 41, S. 641 und Programmheft der Philharmonic Society vom 21. Juni 1875, Mendelssohn habe eine Bearbeitung für Klavier vierhändig dem Londoner Verlag Cramer & Co. erfolglos angeboten, erscheint sehr zweifelhaft. MacFarren nimmt in einer Rezension von 1852 irrtümlich an, die 1851 von Ewer & Co. publizierte Bearbeitung für Klavier vierhändig sei diese mendelssohnsche. Tatsächlich beruht diese Ausgabe auf der im selben Jahr bei Breitkopf & Härtel erschienenen Ausgabe: Symphonie No. 4 für Orchester von Felix Mendelssohn Bartholdy, bearbeitet für Pianoforte zu 4 Hdn., Plattennummer 8361. Diese Bearbeitung stammt von Julius Rietz. Vgl. Verzeichnis des Musikalien-Verlages Breitkopf & Härtel in Leipzig. Vollständig bis Ende 1891, Bd. 1, S. 398.
[15] Siehe unten: Revisionsbericht zu Quelle 2.
[16] Brief von Fanny Hensel vom 18. Juni 1834 in: Citron, Marcia J. (Hg): *The Letters of Fanny Hensel to Felix Mendelssohn*, Pendragon Press 1987, S. 471.

[17] Brief von Fanny Hensel ohne Datum (ca. 1. August 1834) in: Citron, Marcia J. (Hg), ebda., S. 475.
[18] Klingemann, Karl (Hg): *Felix Mendelssohn-Bartholdys Briefwechsel mit Legationsrat Karl Klingemann in London*, Essen 1909, S. 171.
[19] Moscheles, Felix (Hg): *Briefe von Felix Mendelssohn-Bartholdy an Ignaz und Charlotte Moscheles*, Leipzig 1888, S. 150.

liches Versprechen erinnert, den ersten Satz zu überarbeiten:

Die [Direktoren der Philharmonic Society] wünschen zudem, dass ich Sie an die von Ihnen geäußerte Absicht erinnere, einen neuen ersten Satz für Ihre Sinfonie in A zu schreiben, welchen sie sehr gerne bekämen, sobald er vollendet ist. [Original Englisch][20]

Mendelssohn sah sich durch diese Auffordung brüskiert.[21] Das Antwortschreiben Mendelssohns ist selbst nicht erhalten. Auf der Rückseite von Watts' Brief hat er jedoch seine Antwort skizziert:

Auch war ich mir nicht bewusst, dass ich der Philharmonic Society meine Absicht mitgeteilt habe, einen neuen I. Satz für meine Sinfonie in A zu schreiben. Obwohl ich dies einst beabsichtigte, kann ich Ihnen gegenwärtig nicht sagen [ursprünglich: weiß ich nicht] ob und wann ich dies tun werde. [Original Englisch][22]

Daraufhin schrieb Charles Neate einer der Direktoren der Phiharmonic Society an Mendelssohn, um eine Klärung herbeizuführen:

Ich bedaure außerordentlich durch eine Mitteilung von Moscheles herausfinden zu müssen, dass es zwischen Ihnen und der Philharmonischen Gesellschaft wegen Ihrer Sinfonie in A zu einem Missverständnis gekommen ist. Allem Anschein nach waren Sie überrascht von der Frage, ob Sie einen neuen Satz geschrieben hätten. Ich bin über Ihre Überraschung nicht erstaunt, da Sie anscheinend die Unterhaltung mit mir vergessen haben, auf unserem Heimweg von Mrs. Shaw[23] in der Berner Street, als Sie auf meine Bemerkung, dass wir – die Philharmonische – Ihre Sinfonie in A aufführen würden, antworteten: [„,]Nein! Führen Sie sie noch nicht wieder auf, denn ich möchte einen neuen ersten (oder letzten, ich habe vergessen welchen) Satz schreiben["] und daher – wurde sie nicht aufgeführt.[Original Englisch][24]

Auch in diesem Fall ist Mendelssohns Antwort nur auf der Rückseite des Briefes von Neate erhalten:

Ich kenne die Mitteilung Moscheles' nicht, auf die Sie sich anfangs beziehen, aber ich war in der Tat etwas befremdet, von dieser Gesellschaft eine Einladung zu erhalten, dies zu tun. Ich gebe sogar zu, daß Ihr Brief meinen Eindruck in dieser Hinsicht nicht ändert, denn ich bin mir vollkommen bewußt, daß ich früher einmal eine solche Idee hatte; auch denke ich nicht, daß, falls Sie unsere Unterhaltung der Gesellschaft mitgeteilt hätten (wofür sie, denke ich, wirklich nicht gedacht war), dies bewirkt hätte, daß die Aufführungen dieser Sinfonie unterblieben wären, und darüber wäre ich tatsächlich weder befremdet gewesen noch hätte ich mich darüber beklagt. Aber es scheint doch so zu sein, daß weder ich noch Sie diese unsere Unterhaltung als eine Nachricht an die Philharmonische betrachtet haben, denn ein Jahr nachdem [die Unterhaltung] stattgefunden hat, stelle ich fest, daß die Sinfonie von der Philh. Soc. aufgeführt worden ist.[25] Umstände, die Sie anscheinend vergessen haben. Demgemäß, da Sie der Philh. nicht im Juni 1838 erzählt haben, was ich vielleicht Ihnen im September 1837 gesagt haben könnte, so kann es entweder nicht für die Gesell. intendiert gewesen sein oder Sie müssen mir eine gewisse Befremdung zugestehen (daß unsere [Unterhaltung] 1840 erwähnt wird, von der ich die Direktoren nicht direkt unterrichtet habe.)

Aber all dies bezieht sich auf die Einladung zu einem neuen Satz für eine meiner alten Kompositionen, und es ist völlig falsch und weit entfernt von meinen wahren Absichten, wenn Sie in Ihrem Brief davon ausgehen, daß ich irgendwelche Erklärungen wünsche, warum diese Sinfonie nicht aufgeführt wurde. Über eine derartige Angelegenheit werde ich mich niemals beklagen noch Bedauern äußern, denn ich habe es immer als eine natürliche [durchgestrichen: und willkommene] Konsequenz des wahren Wertes einer Komposition angesehen, und Sie werden sich daran erinnern, wie oft ich Ihnen gegenüber und anderen zum Ausdruck gebracht habe, daß ich mit dieser, wie mit vielen andren meiner Kompositionen keineswegs zufrieden bin.[26]

Abgeschlossen wird diese Korrespondenz mit einem entschuldigenden Brief von William

---

[20] Brief von W. Watts vom 20. Okt. 1840 in Bodleian Library, Oxford *(GB-Ob* MS. M. D. M. d. 38, 103), zitiert nach Cooper, John Michael, ebda.

[21] Vgl. Mendelssohns Brief an Klingemann vom 26. Oktober 1840 in: *Felix Mendelssohn-Bartholdys Briefwechsel mit Legationsrat Karl Klingemann in London*, Essen 1909, S. 248–250.

[22] Ebda.

[23] Diese Unterredung fand in der ersten Septemberhälfte 1837 statt nach einem Besuch bei der Altistin Mary Shaw (1814–1876).

[24] Brief vom 18. Jan. 1841 in Bodleian Library, Oxford *(GB-Ob* MS. M. D. M. d. 39, 24) zitiert nach Cooper, John Michael, a.a.O.

[25] Gemeint ist die Aufführung am 18. Juni 1838 unter Moscheles' Leitung.

[26] Bodleian Library, Oxford *(GB-Ob* MS. M. D. M. d. 39, 133), in: Cooper, John Michael, a.a.O.

Watts und Charles Neate vom 19. März 1841.[27] Damit blieb die „Italienische Sinfonie" nicht nur unvollendet, sondern wurde auch in der Folge zu Mendelssohns Lebzeiten nicht mehr aufgeführt. Die erste posthume Aufführung fand auf Wunsch von Königin Victoria am 13. März 1848 durch die Philharmonic Society in London statt. Die erste Aufführung in Deutschland erfolgte nach längerer Vorbereitung am 1. November 1849 im Gewandhaus zu Leipzig. Im Druck veröffentlicht wurde die Partitur in der vollständigen Fassung 1851 bei Breitkopf & Härtel, Leipzig als „Symphonie No. 4 [...], op. 90, Nr. 19 der nachgelassenen Werke" durch das Herausgebergremium von Mendelssohns Nachlass: Ferdinand David, Moritz Hauptmann, Ignaz Moscheles und Julius Rietz.

Die Quellen

Zu Mendelssohns „Italienischer Sinfonie" sind folgende Quellen erhalten.

1. Vollständige autographe Partitur im Besitz der Staatsbibliothek zu Berlin – Preußischer Kulturbesitz: Musikabteilung mit Mendelssohn-Archiv *(D-B* Mus.ms. autogr. Mendelssohn 27, Seite 1–99). (AUT). Zwei Paginierungen. Eine Zählung von fremder Hand beginnend mit dem Titelblatt fortlaufend durch alle vier Sätze. Paginierung hier jeweils nur auf den Recto-Seiten. Eine Zählung von der Hand Mendelssohns nur im I. Satz beginnend auf der Seite 3, gezählt als Seite 1, fortlaufend bis zur Seite 48, gezählt als Seite 44.
Zwei Seiten sind von Mendelssohn mit je einem neuen Blatt überklebt worden, wodurch die ursprünglichen Versionen verdeckt wurden. Die zusammengeklebten Seiten sind in der ersten Paginierung mitgezählt: Am Ende des I. Satzes Takt 98ff. ist die ursprüngliche Version auf Seite 46, die Seite 47 ist unbeschrieben, die Seite 48 bietet die endgültige Version.

Im IV. Satz Takt 97–104 ist die ursprüngliche Version auf Seite 77, die Seite 78 ist unbeschrieben, die Seite 79 bietet die endgültige Version.
Hochformat, 16 Systeme. Verschiedene Papiersorten. Auf dem Titelblatt von der Hand Mendelssohns *Sinfonia für ganzes Orchester,* von fremder Hand der Zusatz *(op. 90).* Seite 2 unbeschrieben, ab Seite 3 fortlaufend beschrieben. Auf Seite 3 links oben *Sinfonia,* rechts oben das Kürzel *H. D. m.* (Hilf Du mir). Die letzte Seite mit der Datierung Mendelssohns *Berlin den 13 März 1833.*
AUT ist die Partitur, welche Mendelssohn für die Uraufführung am 13. Mai 1833 in London verwendete. Die Partitur trägt das Abschlussdatum 13. März 1833. Mendelssohn ließ am 10. April die Partitur in Berlin binden.[28] Zwei Tage nach seiner Ankunft in London am 27. April unterrichtete er die Direktoren der Philharmonic Society davon, dass die Partitur nun zur Verfügung stünde.[29] Am 1. Mai findet sich der Eintrag in Mendelssohns Tagebuch: „Ab[ends] Sinf[onia] fertig durchgesehen", am 11. Mai, am Tag der ersten Probe, der Eintrag: „früh Stimmen d[urchge]sehen".[30] Die Partitur verblieb nach der Uraufführung in London, möglicherweise zunächst im Besitz der Philharmonic Society. Später bewahrte lgnaz Moscheles sie auf, wie aus einem Brief Moscheles' an Mendelssohn aus dem Jahr 1837 hervorgeht.[31] Später erhielt Mendelssohn, der genaue Zeitpunkt ist nicht bekannt, die Partitur zurück. Sie

---

27 Ebda.

28 Vgl. Brief Mendelssohns vom 10. April 18[33] in: Klingemann, Karl (Hg.): *Felix Mendelssohn-Bartholdys Briefwechsel mit Legationsrat Karl Klingemann in London,* Essen 1909, S. 115.

29 Brief an William Watts in: Foster, Myles B.: *History of the Philharmonic Society of London,* London 1912, S. 118; Hogarth, George: *The Philharmonic Society of London,* London 1862, S. 60.

30 Tagebuch: in Bodleian Library, Oxford *(GB-Ob* MS. M. D. M. g. 4), zitiert nach Cooper, John Michael, ebda.

31 Brief vom 23. Dez. 1837 in: Moscheles, Felix (Hg.): *Briefe von Felix Mendelssohn-Bartholdy an Ignaz und Charlotte Moscheles,* Leipzig 1888, S. 150.

findet sich in der von ihm 1844 geschriebenen Liste seiner eigenen Musikalien.[32]

2. Autographe Skizzen im Besitz der Bodleian Library, Oxford *(GB-Ob* MS. M. D. M. b. 5, Fols. 136r–146v). Folierung von fremder Hand. Diese Skizzen enthalten in vollständiger Partitur Material zum I., III. und IV. Satz. Sie sind AUT unmittelbar zuzuordnen und sind möglicherweise während einer Überarbeitung von AUT entstanden.[33]

3. Handschriftliche Kopie im Besitz der British Library, London als Leihgabe der Royal Philharmonic Society *(GB-Lbm* Loan 4/290). Keine Folierung oder Paginierung (160 Seiten). (BL).
Querformat, 16 Systeme. Auf den Seiten 1–44 ist links unten aufgedruckt *W. GOODWIN, 4, UPPER WELLINGTON ST.,* rechts unten *COVENT GARDEN.* Auf dem Titelblatt *Sinfonie No 4* (ursprünglich *Sinfonie No 2)* Mendelssohn Score 1848. Ab Seite 2–158 fortlaufend beschrieben.
Am Ende der Sätze jeweils eine unbeschriebene Seite.
Handschrift des Kopisten William Goodwin. Korrekturen und Zusätze von William Sterndale Bennett. Auf Seite 33 ist ein Teil des Notentextes ergänzt mit dem Zusatz *? something wanted WSB.*
BL ist eine Abschrift, welche die Philharmonic Society für die erste posthume Aufführung der „Italienischen Sinfonie" am 13. März 1848 in London herstellen ließ. In den *Directors Minutes* der Gesellschaft findet sich am 13. Februar 1848 der Eintrag: „es wurde angeordnet, daß eine Partitur von Mendelssohns Sinfonie in A, Nr. 2, unverzüglich angefertigt

werde"[34]. Am folgenden Tag wurde der Kopist William Goodwin durch den Sekretär der Gesellschaft G. W. Budd beauftragt, eine solche Kopie zu erstellen: „Die Direktoren wünschen bis zum nächsten Sonntag eine Partitur von Mendelssohns Symphony in A – No 2 anfertigen zu lassen. Wenn Sie sie mir am Samstag spät noch zustellen, genügt es.[35] Die Direktoren haben die Partitur fristgerecht erhalten. In den *Directors Minutes* findet sich am 20. Februar 1848 folgende Anweisung für einen Brief an William Goodwin: „Die Direktoren sind sehr zufrieden mit der Pünktlichkeit, mit der Sie die Sinfonie geschickt haben".[36] Die Vorlage für die Abschrift Goodwins kann nicht AUT gewesen sein, da sich die originale Partitur zu diesem Zeitpunkt in Mendelssohns Nachlass in Leipzig befand. Es ist daher nur möglich, dass diese Abschrift aus den Orchesterstimmen der Uraufführung, welche Eigentum der Philharmonic Society waren, spartiert wurde. Der Verbleib dieser Orchesterstimmen ist jedoch unbekannt.[37]

4. Revidierte autographe Partitur des II., III. und IV. Satzes im Besitz der Staatsbibliothek zu Berlin – Preußischer Kulturbesitz: Musikabteilung mit Mendelssohn-Archiv *(D-B* Mus. ms. autogr. Mendelssohn 28, Seite 5–58).
Paginierung von fremder Hand, jeweils nur auf den Recto-Seiten. Eine Seite ist von Mendelssohn mit einem neuen Blatt überklebt worden, wodurch die ursprüng-

[32] „Mendelssohn's 1844 List of his Music", in: Jones, Peter Ward (Hg.): *Catalogue of the Mendelssohn Papers in the Bodleian Library*, Oxford, Bd. III, S. 292.

[33] Eine eingehende Bewertung und Beschreibung dieser Skizzen bietet Cooper, John Michael in: „,Aber eben dieser Zweifel': A New Look at Mendelssohn's ‚Italian' Symphony", in: *19th Century Music*, Bd. 15, Nr. 3 (1992), S. 169–187.

[34] Im Besitz der British Library, London als Leihgabe der Royal Philharmonic Society (Loan 48. 2. 4. (1848)).

[35] Eintrag am 14. Februar 1848 im Kopierbuch der Philharmonic Society im Besitz der British Library, London, als Leihgabe der Royal Philharmonic Society: Copies of Letters 1846–49; Loan 48. 6. 2.

[36] Im Besitz der British Library, London, als Leihgabe der Royal Philharmonic Society (Loan 48. 2. 4. (1848)).

[37] Vgl. zu dieser Handschrift Ward Jones, Peter: „Mendelssohn Scores in the Library of the Philharmonic Society", in: Schmidt, Christian Martin (Hg): *Felix Mendelssohn Bartholdy*, Kongress-Bericht Berlin, 1994; Wiesbaden/ Leipzig/Paris 1997, S. 64–75.

liche Version verdeckt wurde. Die zusammengeklebten Seiten sind in der Paginierung mitgezählt: Im II. Satz Takt 77ff. ist die ursprüngliche Version auf Seite 10, die Seite 11 ist unbeschrieben, die Seite 12 bietet die endgültige Version. Hochformat, 16 Systeme. Auf der Seite 5 rechts oben das Kürzel *H. D. m.* (Hilf Du mir).

Diese revidierte Partitur entstand im Juni 1834 in Düsseldorf. Am 26. Juni 1834 schreibt Mendelssohn an Ignaz und Charlotte Moscheles:

Diese Tage kam der Dr. Franck, den Du kennst, nach Düsseldorf, und ich wünschte ihm einiges aus meiner A dur-Sinfonie zeigen zu können; da ich sie nun nicht habe, so fing ich an, das Andante wieder aufzuschreiben, und kam dabei gleich an so viele errrata, daß mich's interessirte, und ich auch das Menuet und das Finale aufschrieb, aber mit vielen sehr nöthigen Verbesserungen, und wenn mir solch eine Stelle auffiel, so mußte ich immer an Dich denken, der Du mir niemals ein tadelndes Wort darüber gesagt, und das Alles doch gewiß deutlicher und besser gewußt hast, als ich jetzt. Nur das erste Stück habe ich nicht dazu geschrieben, denn wenn ich da mal drüber komme, so fürchte ich, ich muß vom 4ten Takt an das ganze Thema verändern, und somit ziemlich das ganze erste Stück, wozu ich aber jetzt keine Zeit habe. Mir scheint die Dominante im 4ten Takt ganz unangenehm; ich glaube es muß die Septime (a, g) sein.[38]

Auch in einem Brief an Klingemann zwei Tage später erwähnt Mendelssohn diese Revision des II., III. und IV. Satzes der Partitur: „Als ich Deine freundlichen Worte über meine Sinfonie las, machte ich mich sogleich daran für Franck die drei letzten Stücke aufzuschreiben und umzuarbeiten, ich wollt', ich könnte sie Dir eben vorspielen, sie sind viel besser geworden. Namentlich Nr. 2 und 3."[39]

Wie aus dem Brief an Ignaz und Charlotte Moscheles hervorgeht, hat Mendelssohn eine Revision des I. Satzes zu diesem Zeitpunkt noch nicht beabsichtigt. Dem entspricht auch sein Kürzel *H. D. m.* auf der Seite 5 der Partitur, mit welchem Mendelssohn jeweils den Beginn einer kompositorischen Arbeit kennzeichnet.[40]

Editionsprinzipien

Mendelssohn hat die Komposition seiner „Italienischen Sinfonie" nicht vollendet. Er hat dieses Werk entgegen seiner ursprünglichen Absicht nicht im Druck veröffentlicht. Die geplante vollständige Revision wurde von ihm nur teilweise ausgeführt. Aufgrund der erhaltenen Quellen ist nicht eindeutig zu entscheiden, ob die Überarbeitung des II., III. und IV. Satzes die endgültige Fassung dieser drei Sätze darstellt. Mendelssohn hat die revidierte Teilpartitur aus dem Jahr 1834 nicht zur Aufführung gebracht. Auch ist nicht zu rekonstruieren, in welchem Umfang Mendelssohn den I. Satz der Sinfonie überarbeiten oder möglicherweise sogar neu schreiben wollte. Der erhaltene Briefwechsel mit der Philharmonic Society aus den Jahren 1840/1841 macht jedoch deutlich, dass Mendelssohn diese Sinfonie, welche er im Konzert der Öffentlichkeit schon vorgestellt hatte, nicht ausdrücklich verworfen hat, auch wenn er weitere Aufführungen nicht unterstützte. Die vorliegende Ausgabe bietet die „Italienische Sinfonie" in dieser im Konzertsaal veröffentlichten „Londoner" Fassung. Damit entspricht sie grundsätzlich der als „Symphonie No. 4 [...], op. 90, Nr. 19 der nachgelassenen Werke" 1851 herausgegebenen Version.

Entsprechend dieser Bewertung bildet AUT die Grundlage für die vorliegende Ausgabe unter ergänzender Berücksichtigung von BL. Die re-

---

[38] Moscheles, Felix (Hg.), ebda., S. 95/96.
[39] Brief an Klingemann vom 26. Juni 1834 in: Klingemann, Karl (Hg.), ebda., S. 135.

[40] Eine philologische Bewertung dieser Handschrift bieten: Cooper, John Michael: „,Aber eben dieser Zweifel': A New Look at Mendelssohn's ‚Italian' Symphony", in: *19th Century Music*, Bd. 15, Nr. 3 (1992), S. 169–187 und Konold, Wulf: *Die Symphonien Felix Mendelssohn Bartholdys – Untersuchungen zu Werkgestalt und Formstruktur*, Laaber 1992, S. 394–413.

vidierte Partitur des II., III. und IV. Satzes aus dem Jahr 1834 wurde nicht verwendet, um eine eklektische Ausgabe zu vermeiden.

Die Position der Phrasierungsbögen und der dynamischen und agogischen Bezeichnungen in AUT ist aufgrund der flüchtigen Schreibweise und der zahlreichen Retuschen häufig nicht eindeutig. Auf diese Stellen wird in den Einzelanmerkungen hingewiesen.

In gleicher Weise ist die Phrasierung, Dynamik und Agogik in vielen Fällen nicht einheitlich. Diese Schreibweise Mendelssohns ist grundsätzlich beibehalten worden.

Die in AUT und BL verwendeten Staccatostriche werden in der vorliegenden Ausgabe als schlanke Keile (ʼ) wiedergegeben. In einigen wenigen Fällen wurde die Setzung der Staccatopunkte und Staccatostriche vereinheitlicht. Diese sind in den Einzelanmerkungen verzeichnet. Auf die Stellen, an denen die Unterscheidung zwischen Staccatopunkt und Staccatostrich in AUT nicht eindeutig ist, wird ebenfalls in den Einzelanmerkungen hingewiesen.

Boris von Haken

Einzelanmerkungen

AUT = Autographe Partitur, *D-B* Mus.ms.autogr.Mendelssohn 27
BL = Handschriftliche Kopie, *GB-Lbm* Loan 4/290

Satz I

Im Instrumentenspiegel *Bassi* für Violoncello und Contrabbasso in AUT, Violoncello/Basso in BL

Takt 6–7	Vl.I, II Phrasierung mehrdeutig in AUT, ebenso in den analogen Takten 54–55/372–373
23–30	Ob.1, 2 Stimmen fehlen in BL
31	Fg.1 *p* statt *f* in BL
49	Vc., Cb. *cresc.* in AUT und BL
68–69	Timp. Pause in BL
92–94/	Cl.1, 2, Fg.1, 2, Vc., Cb. Phrasierung nach BL, Phrasierungsbögen wegen
96–98	Korrekturen mehrdeutig in AUT
110	Cl.1 *Solo* in BL
188	Cl.l *dolce* in BL
189–190	Ob.1 *Solo espressivo* in BL
171	Vc., Cb. *f* in AUT und BL
184	Fl.l, 2 *f/sf* in AUT
199a	Vla. *a 2* für *div.* in AUT
207a	Vla. *unis.* ab 2. Achtel in BL
217–218	Vc., Cb. Phrasierung nach BL,
	Phrasierungsbogen von c¹ zu d in AUT
231	Ob.1, 2 *pp* in AUT und BL
279	Fl.1, 2 *ff* nach BL
345	Ob.1 *Solo* in BL
376	Vla., Vc., Cb. ursprünglich *mp* in AUT, *mf* in BL
404	Fl.1 *Solo pp* in BL
405	Cl.1 *Solo pp* in BL
456	Fl.1, 2 *Solo* in BL
460	Ob.1, 2 *Solo* in BL
	Vla., Vc. *p* in BL
517	Vla. *a 2* in AUT, keine Anweisung in BL
517–519	Vla. keine Phrasierungsbögen in BL

Satz II

Takt 11	Fl.1, 2 *Soli* in BL
12–13	Fl.1 Phrasierung mehrdeutig in AUT, in BL Fragezeichen über dem System
19	Vc., Cb. Staccatozeichen mehrdeutig in AUT, Staccatopunkte in BL
23–24	Vc., Cb. Staccatostriche in AUT, Staccatopunkte in BL
27	Fl.2 Dynamik nach BL, unleserlich in AUT
	Vc., Cb. Staccatopunkt in BL
30	Fl.1 Dynamik unleserlich in AUT, keine Bezeichnung in BL
47	Fl.1 Phrasierungsbogen bis 5. Achtel in AUT
	Vl.1 Phrasierungsbogen bis 3. Viertel in AUT

SYMPHONY No. 4
'Italian'

Felix Mendelssohn Bartholdy
(1809–1847)
Op. 90

I. **Allegro vivace**

Flauto 1 2

Oboe 1 2

Clarinetto (A) 1 2

Fagotto 1 2

Corno (A) 1 2

Tromba (D) 1 2

Timpani (A, E)

Violino I

Violino II

Viola

Violoncello

Contrabbasso

Edited by Boris von Haken
© 2014 Ernst Eulenburg Ltd, London
and Ernst Eulenburg & Co GmbH, Mainz

4

6

8

10

14

20

26

30

40

48

50

52

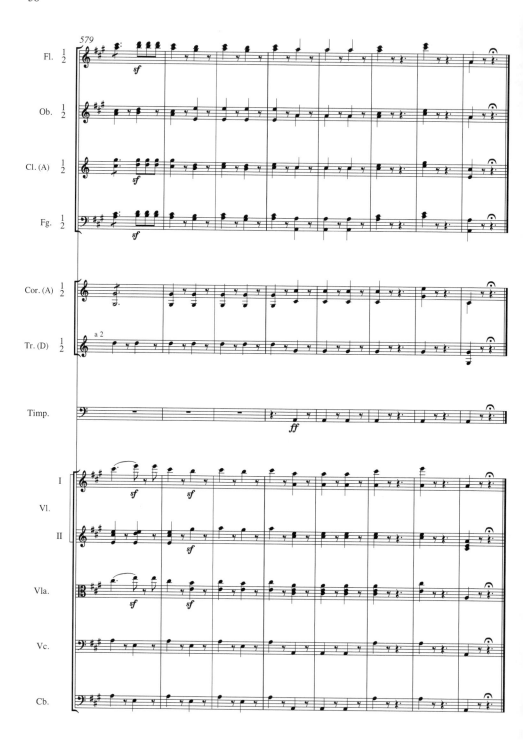

II. Andante con moto

68

III. Con moto moderato

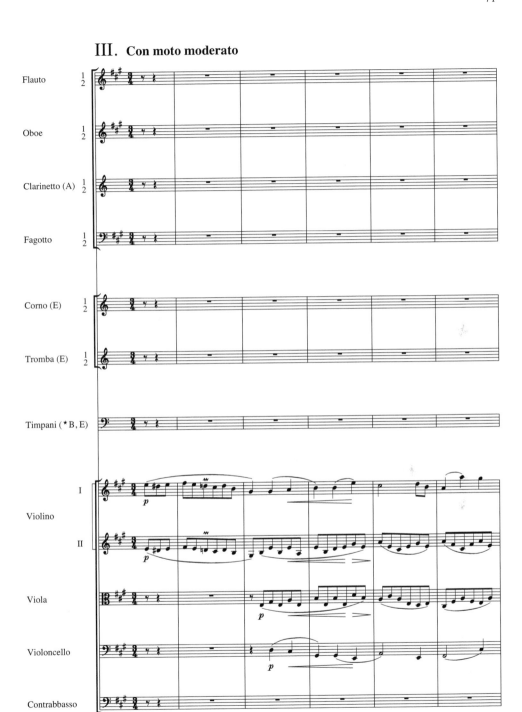

★ B = German/deutsch H

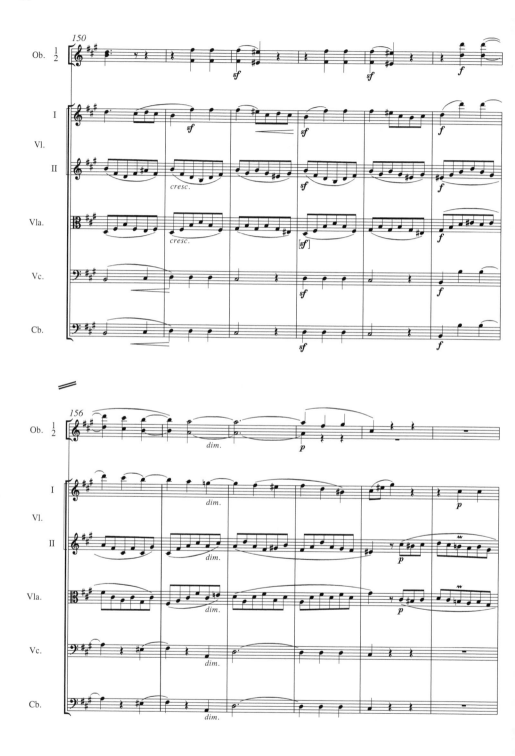

Coda

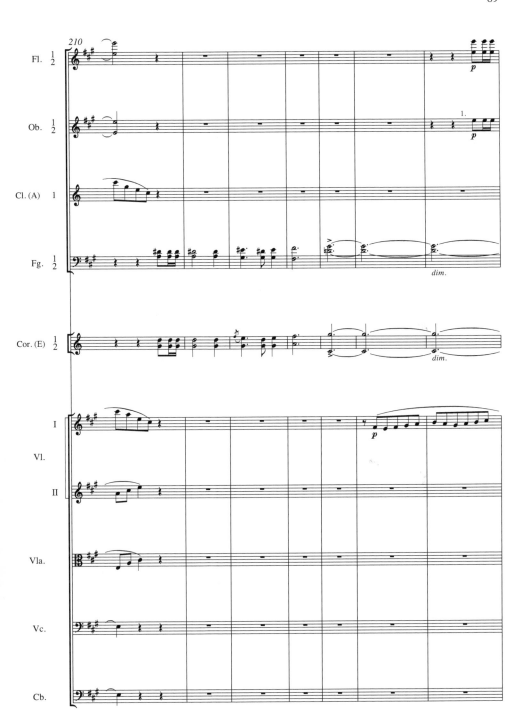

IV. Saltarello. Presto

112

114

118

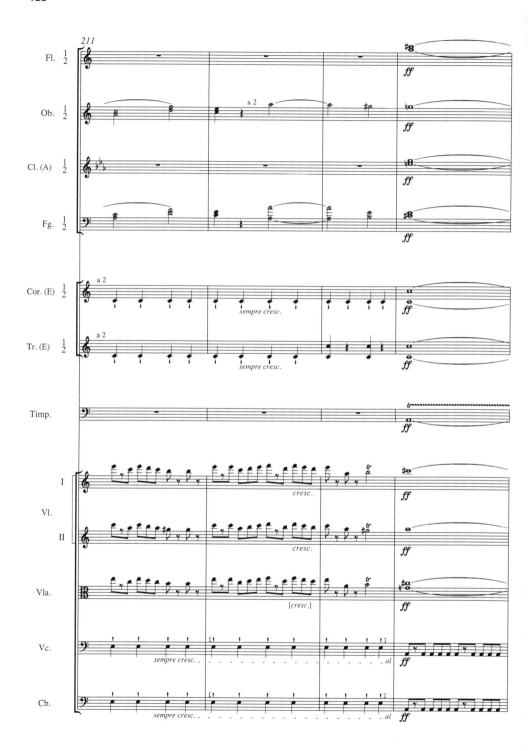

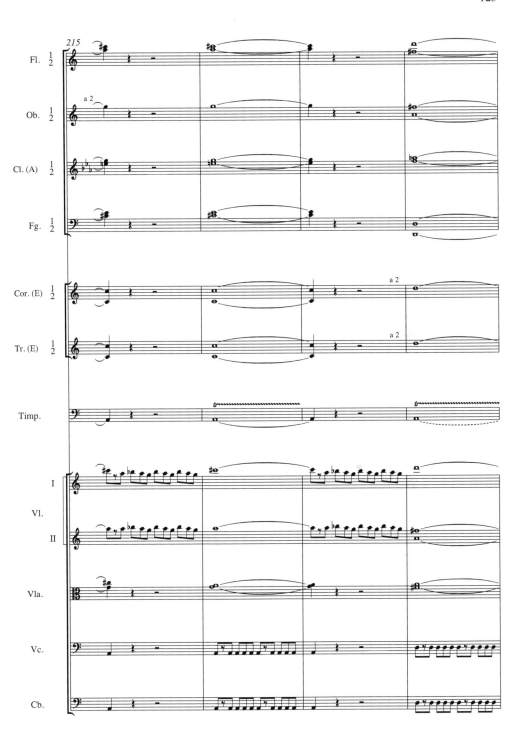

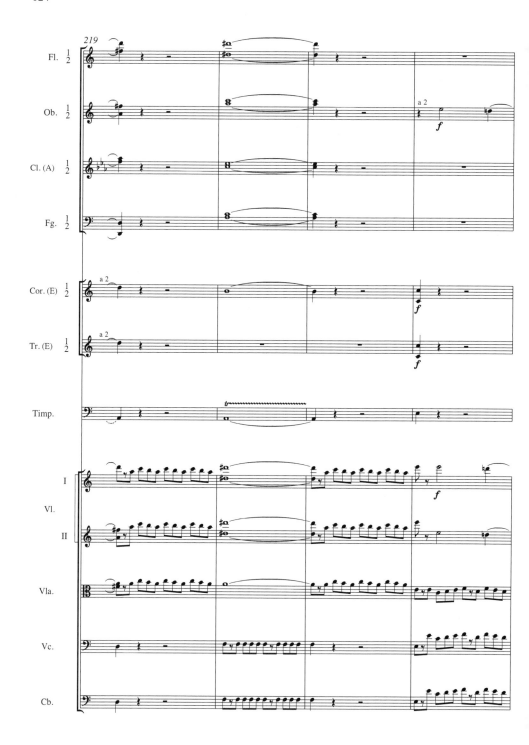